A Letter from Fish Bay

Joy Cowley

photographs by Terry Coles

Learning Media

Contents

1. Welcome to Fish Bay

Dear Friends,

I live with my husband, Terry Coles, in Fish Bay. That's at the top of the South Island of New Zealand. It's a long, long way from ice cream. That means we have to make our own, but it's not the same as chocolate ripple or strawberry in a cone.

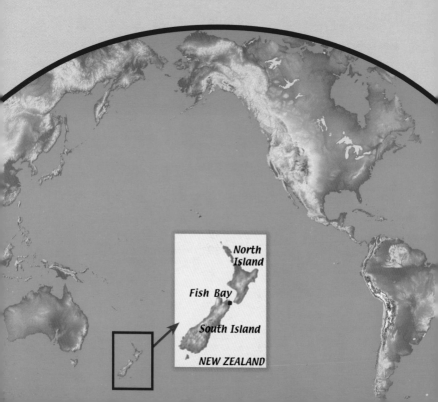

North Island

Fish Bay

South Island

NEW ZEALAND

When we go into town, we buy two large ice creams and eat them quickly before they melt.

Picton is our nearest town, but about three miles away, in Waitaria Bay, there's a school full of friends who sometimes help me with my writing.

People ask us if we are ever lonely living so far away from town. The answer is "No!"

When we're not visiting people, or being visited by them, we have the company of eight cats, seven hens, about a hundred sheep, and *lots* of birds.

In this bay, there are tuis, bellbirds, fantails, cuckoos, herons, ducks, swamp hens, and cormorants like the one in this picture.

What do I do all day? Well, there's always plenty to do.

Some mornings I go fishing.
I get mullet or sole or snapper,
or sometimes, all three.

Other mornings,
I work in the
garden, growing
flowers and fruit
and vegetables.

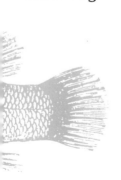

My favorite flowers are roses.
I have about two hundred
old rose bushes with
scented blooms.

The bees love them.
You have to look
carefully before you put
your nose into one of my roses.

After breakfast, I shut myself in my office, and I write until about three o'clock. I used to write stories with a pen and a pad. These days, I use a computer.

But I still take a pen and pad with me when I travel. I never know when a story is going to pop into my head.

In the late afternoon, Terry and I feed the hens and the eight yowling cats.

The cats' names are Bill, Dick, Maggie, Tui, Pango, Huggie, Lucky, and Marmite. They are all purry cats, and they love to be cuddled.

Often there is time to do some spinning or knitting with wool from our sheep.

Sometimes, I play with the train set in my office.

Terry and I take turns to cook the meal in the evening. We both enjoy cooking and eating.

Our food is mostly from the sea and land – oysters, mussels, fish, fresh vegetables, and fruit, as well

as Terry's homemade bread. But there are some foods that we buy in town.

We go into town every three weeks. It takes two and a half hours to get there and another two and a half hours to get home again. That doesn't leave us much time for shopping.

Our mail comes every day, and we have a phone and a fax machine, so we are in touch with the rest of New Zealand and the world.

My mail is interesting, but there's so much of it. I need a bigger mailbox.

2. Thousands of Letters!

Nearly every day, I get bundles of letters from schools all around the world. Some weeks I get more than a thousand letters!

It's lovely to get so much mail, but I do have a problem. Can you guess what it is? Yes! I have trouble answering all these letters.

I always try to write back, but I never seem to catch up, and I know that you're disappointed when you don't hear from me for a long time.

So here, I want to say "thank you" for all your great letters. I also want to say "sorry" if you've had to wait for a reply.

Many of your letters ask questions. I'm writing down some of the things that I'm often asked, and the answers.

★ *When did you start writing?*

I can't remember. I've always liked writing and telling stories. I was the eldest of five children.

At night, I used to tell my sisters long adventure stories that went on week after week.

This is me on the right, aged five. I'm with my sisters, Joan and Heather.

I started writing for children in the 1960s, when my own four children were young. From that, I became very interested in writing for children who were learning to read. I also used to write stories for adults.

★ *What do you like best – writing for children or adults?*

I really prefer writing for children.
My adult writing is very serious.
My children's writing is usually funny.
I don't know why this is, but it probably explains why I get more pleasure from writing for children.

★ *How many books have you written?*

I don't know. There must be more than five hundred books for children.
I've written only nine books for adults.

★ *Where do you get your ideas?*

From all kinds of things. Many ideas for children's stories come from children themselves. For example, one day, a six-year-old friend was telling me about his cat, who was very big.

"What's he called?" I asked.
My friend said, "He's got a proper
name, but I can't remember it.
We just call him Greedy Cat."

Can you guess which story came
from that?

Another time, I'd been fishing and
I was very cold. I got into a hot bath.
The water seemed to make a noise like
"wishy-washy, wishy-washy." I thought,
"Now, that sounds nice. Perhaps it
could go into a story." All at once, a
cow and a pig and a duck jumped into
my head. And that's how the story of
Mrs. Wishy-washy began.

One day, some children came to see me after school. We had some milk and  cookies, but there was no cake in the house. Someone said it would be good fun if we could make the biggest cake in the whole wide world. We talked about the things we'd need for such an enormous cake. And *there* was another story. So you see, stories can come from anywhere.

★ *How many times do you write a story?*

Usually four or five times. When I write the first draft, I get the story down as fast as possible. I don't worry too much about mistakes. That's me being an author.

But a writer must be a mixture
of two people – author and editor.
Once the story is written, I become an
editor. I go over it again and again,
making corrections.

When a story is as good as I can make
it, I put it away for a few days. Then
I look at it again, and
I usually see some
more mistakes.

So, I write the story a
fourth and perhaps a
fifth time. That's me
being an editor.

You'll find that
with your own
stories; you'll
have to be an
author and
editor, too.

Greedy Cat

Mum went to ~~town~~ *shop*
and got some *saus*
Along *~~In~~* came Greedy Ca
He looked in Mum'.
Gobble, gobble, gob
a *And* that was the en

Mum went to ~~town~~ *shopping*
and got some *chocola*
Along *~~In~~* came Greedy Cat.
He looked in **Mum's bag**
Gobble, gobble, gobble.
a *And* that was the end of t

Mum went to ~~town~~ *shopping*
and got some potato chips.
Along *~~In~~* came Greedy Cat.
He looked in **Mum's bag**. *the s*
Gobble, gobble, goble.
a *And* that was the end of that.

Mum went to ~~town~~ *shopping*
and got some peanuts. *chocolate .*
Along *~~In~~* came Greedy Cat.
He looked in **Mum's bag**. *the shopping ba*
Gobble, gobble, gobble.
and *And* that was the end of that.

★ *What story is your favorite?*

I have several favorites.
There's *Uncle Joe* and *Old
Tuatara*. Greedy Cat is a
favorite because I love Robyn
Belton's pictures.

★ *Who is your favorite children's author?*

My favorite author of children's books is Margaret Mahy. She can be serious or funny, or both in the same book, and she often uses delicious words.

★ *Do you draw your own pictures?*

No, I don't. Those are done by artists who have had a lot of experience in illustrating books.

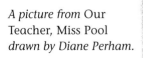

A picture from The Smile drawn by Clare Bowes.

A picture from Our Teacher, Miss Pool drawn by Diane Perham.

★ *How many children do you have?*

There are four children who are grown up now. They are Sharon, Edward, Judith, and James. We are all very close friends. I have four granddaughters – Aja, Lucy, Charlotte, and Phoebe. My five grandsons are Richard, Oscar, Max, Edwin, and Timothy.

This is me and my daughter, Judith, and my grandchildren, Edwin, Oscar, and Max

★ *What is your favorite color?*

Red!

★ *What is your favorite animal?*

I like all animals, including spiders and cockroaches and snakes. Every creature has its own beauty.

★ *What is your favorite food?*

Ice cream!

There! That answers the questions
I usually get from children.

Thank you again for all the beautiful
drawings and letters. They give me a
really warm feeling, like being hugged.

Love from your friend,

Joy Cowley

Joy Cowley

3. A Recipe for Ice Cream

If you would like to make some of Joy Cowley's strawberry ice cream, try this recipe. You will need:

* ★ 1 cup of condensed milk
* ★ 1 cup of cream
* ★ 1 cup of mashed strawberries

Beat the condensed milk, cream, and strawberries together. Pour the mixture into a container.

Put the container into the freezer. When the ice cream is half frozen (after about two hours), beat the mixture again.

Put it back in the freezer and leave it until it's frozen.

If you want to make different flavors of ice cream, you can replace the strawberries with mashed kiwifruit, raspberries, or peaches. A cup of mashed bananas and some chocolate chips is yummy too.